Complete Guide to Chinese Characters

LIVING LANGUAGE®

Published in the United States by Living Language, an imprint of Random House, Inc.

www.livinglanguage.com

Editor: Erin Quirk
Production Editor: Ciara Robinson
Production Manager: Tom Marshall
Interior Design: Sophie Chin
Illustrations: Sophie Chin

First Edition

ISBN: 978-0-307-97177-7

Library of Congress Cataloging-in-Publication Data is available upon request.

This book is available at special discounts for bulk purchases for sales promotions or premiums. Special editions, including personalized covers, excerpts of existing books, and corporate imprints, can be created in large quantities for special needs. For more information, write to Special Markets/ Premium Sales, 1745 Broadway, MD 3-1, New York, New York 10019 or e-mail specialmarkets@ randomhouse.com.

PRINTED IN THE UNITED STATES OF AMERICA

10 9 8 7 6 5 4 3 2 1

Acknowledgments

Thanks to the Living Language team: Amanda D'Acierno, Christopher Warnasch, Suzanne McQuade, Laura Riggio, Erin Quirk, Amanda Munoz, Fabrizio LaRocca, Siobhan O'Hare, Sophie Chin, Sue Daulton, Alison Skrabek, Carolyn Roth, Ciara Robinson, and Tom Marshall.

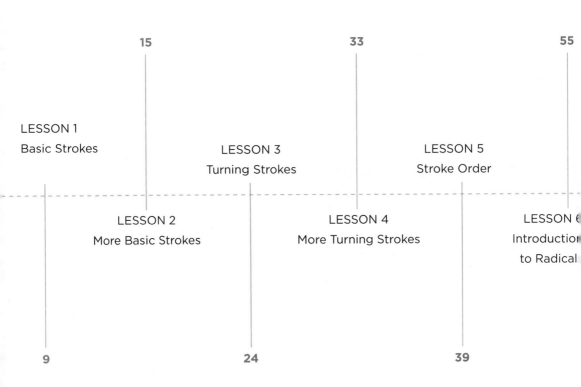
COURSE

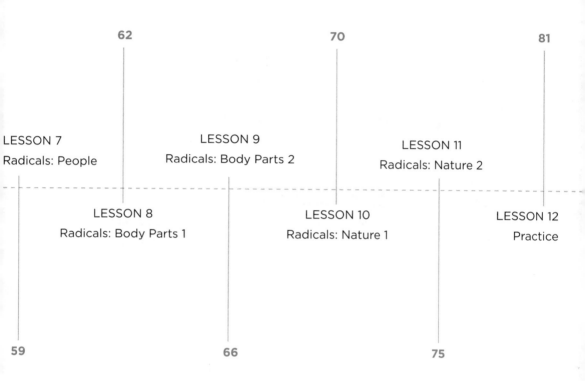
OUTLINE

Introduction:
Characters and Pīnyīn

The goal of this guide is to teach you the essentials for reading and writing in Mandarin Chinese so that you can write and decipher almost any Chinese character on your own, well beyond the specific characters presented here.

In this guide, we will start with the basics of writing Chinese characters and then move on to reading individual characters, full sentences, and short paragraphs.

CHINESE CHARACTERS

Written Chinese is made up of a system of characters rather than an alphabet. There are tens of thousands of Chinese characters, but only about 4,000 of them are actually used in everyday literature and conversation. Of those 4,000 characters, approximately 2,500 of them are considered the most frequently used. A Chinese college graduate generally knows about 4,000 characters, while elementary school students are required to learn about 2,000 characters over the span of six years.

Of course, 2,000 – 4,000 characters probably still seems like quite a lot. However, don't get discouraged. Chinese characters are made up of smaller components that help you to figure out meaning and/or pronunciation. And there are only about 200 of those smaller components. You will learn more about them in Part 2.

In this guide, we will be teaching the simplified form of Chinese characters, which is the standard in mainland China. You'll learn more about simplified characters in Part 1.

PĪNYĪN

Pīnyīn is a system that uses the Latin alphabet to represent the sounds in standard Mandarin Chinese. It was devised for people who do not read hànzì (*Chinese characters*) to read Chinese sounds. In fact, hànzì itself is an example of a pīnyīn word. It is a transliteration, or Latin version, of 汉字. It tells you that 汉字 is pronounced hànzì.

In this course, almost all Chinese words will be written, or at least introduced, in both characters and pīnyīn. However, please keep in mind that sometimes the sounds of certain pīnyīn letters are different from the sounds of those same letters in English. For example, the ì in hànzì is pronounced like the r in thunder. For more information on how to read pīnyīn, see the Pronunciation and Pīnyīn Guide at the back of your *Essential Chinese* book, or your *Intermediate Chinese* or *Advanced Chinese* books if you purchased *Complete Chinese* or *Platinum Chinese*.

Ready? Let's get started!

Part 1: Writing

In this first part of the guide, you will get a comprehensive introduction to writing Chinese characters.

SIMPLIFIED VS. TRADITIONAL CHARACTERS

As you know, this course teaches the simplified form of Chinese characters, which is the standard way of writing Chinese characters in mainland China, Singapore, and Malaysia. In general, simplified characters were developed by reducing the number of brushstrokes in Traditional Chinese characters, which are mainly used in Hong Kong, Taiwan, Macau, and other Chinese-speaking communities in Southeast Asia.

BRUSHSTROKES

Brushstrokes are the different kinds of markings, or strokes, that make up each individual Chinese character. Part 1 is an introduction to the different strokes and the order in which they are put down when writing. Fortunately, there is a limited number of strokes, and a clearly defined order in which to write them. By learning the strokes and the order, you will know how to write almost any Chinese character.

Each stroke has a name. These names are not part of the pronunciation of the character itself. Instead, they are used when someone is trying to describe how a character is written.

TYPES OF BRUSHSTROKES

There are two categories of strokes: "basic" and "turning." Think of "basic" strokes as ones that only take about one movement of the brush or pen to write, while "turning" (also known as "combined") strokes are ones that require the brush or pen to make one or more turns on the paper.

Lesson 1

Basic Strokes

Each Chinese character is built upon a series of brushstrokes. Traditionally, there have been five strokes that are considered to be fundamental. All of the other strokes can be regarded as variations of these five. Here are the names of those five strokes:

1. héng 横
2. shù 竖
3. piě 撇
4. diǎn 点
5. zhé 折

Chinese brushstrokes must be written the correct way in order to be legible. This is actually similar to English. In school, you're usually taught to write an English letter in a specific way, with your pen or pencil moving in a certain direction. If you don't, the letter often looks strange and oddly shaped. Well, Chinese works the same way. As a result, you will see arrows within each stroke to indicate the direction in which your pen should move.

Now let's look at each stroke and see how it's written.

1. HÉNG 横

The héng stroke is one horizontal line that goes from left to right. You can find this stroke in the character 三 sān (*three*).

In fact, as you can see, 三 sān is made up of three héng strokes in a row.

Now practice writing the héng stroke a few times by tracing the stroke in the boxes below. Remember to write it from left to right.

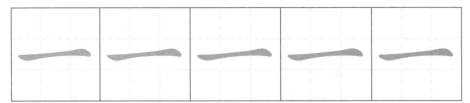

2. SHÙ 竖

The shù stroke goes from top to bottom. You can find this stroke in the character 十 shí *(ten)*.

Notice that 十 shí is made up of a héng stroke and a shù stroke.

Now practice writing the shù stroke a few times by tracing the stroke in the boxes below. Remember to go from top to bottom.

Here are some more sample characters that only consist of héng and shù:

一	二	干
yī	èr	gān
one	*two*	*dry*

3. PIĔ 撇

Piĕ goes from top to bottom left. You can find it in the character 千 qiān (*thousand*).

Notice that piĕ can be tilted either more horizontally, as it is in 千, or more vertically, depending on the character.

Now let's practice. Trace the stroke in the boxes below, remembering to go from top to bottom.

4. DIĂN 点

Diăn is a "dot" that goes from top left to bottom right or top right to bottom left. You can find it in the character 玉 yù (*jade*).

You can also find it in the character 小 xiăo (*small*). In this character, you can actually see two diăn: one going both top right to bottom left and another going from top left to bottom right.

Let's practice. Remember to write from top left to bottom right, or top right to bottom left.

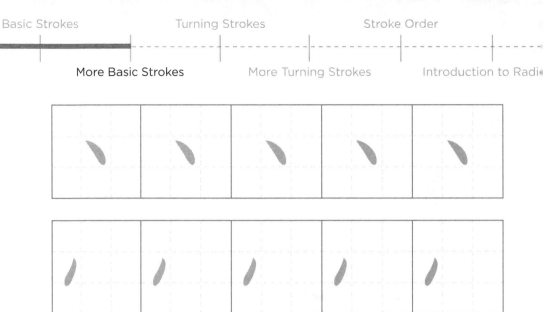

5. ZHÉ 折

Zhé goes horizontally from left to right, with a downwards left hook at the end. It is sometimes also known as the hénggōu stroke, since it is essentially made up of the horizontal héng stroke plus a gōu (*hook*).

You can find the zhé/hénggōu stroke in the character 买 mǎi (*buy*).

Now let's practice. Don't forget to go from left to right, and then at the end, hook to the left.

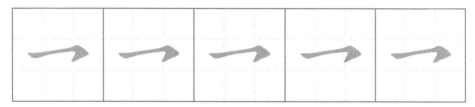

Exercise

In Chinese, it is very important to know the number of strokes in a character. Characters are often organized by number of strokes, such as in the index of a dictionary.

Can you identify the number of strokes in each of the following characters?

CHARACTER	NUMBER OF STROKES
1. 千 qiān (*thousand*)	
2. 干 gān (*dry*)	
3. 玉 yù (*jade*)	

ANSWER KEY:
1. three; 2. three; 3. five

Lesson 2

More Basic Strokes

In this lesson, we'll look at a few more basic strokes. These strokes are slight variations of the five fundamental strokes you learned in Lesson 1.

1. tí 提
2. shùgōu 竖钩
3. shùtí 竖提
4. xiégōu 斜钩
5. nà 捺

Remember that the names of the strokes only exist to identify the strokes. They aren't related to the pronunciation of the character itself.

Now let's take a closer look at each of the strokes mentioned above.

6. Tí 提

The tí stroke goes from bottom left to top right. Note that the length of the stroke and the degree of the tilt can vary; it can be longer or shorter than what's shown above, and more horizontal.

The tí stroke appears as part of the character 冰 bīng (ice).

An example of a longer, more horizontal form of tí can be found in the character 虫 chóng (*worm, insect*).

Now practice writing the tí stroke by tracing the strokes in the boxes below. Don't forget to move your pen from bottom left to top right.

7. SHÙGŌU 竖钩

Shùgōu is the vertical shù stroke from Lesson 1, plus a gōu (*hook*). In other words, go from top to bottom and then add an upwards left hook at the end.

Since the hook is the only difference between the shù stroke and the shùgōu stroke, it can make a big difference if you forget to include it. For example, take a look at the characters 于 yú (*on, in, at, to*) and 干 gān (*dry*).

于 yú

干 gān

Notice that the only difference between 于 yú and 干 gān is that 于 contains the shùgōu stroke while 干 contains the shù stroke.

Just by adding a hook, you change the meaning from *on* to *dry*.

Here are some other Chinese characters that contain the shùgōu stroke:

你	子	小
nǐ	zǐ	xiǎo
You	*son*	*small*

It is also important to note that there is a curved form of the shùgōu stroke known as the wāngōu stroke:

You can see it in the character 狗 gǒu (*dog*):

Now practice writing the shùgōu and wāngōu strokes a few times by tracing the strokes in the boxes below. Don't forget to go from top to bottom and then at the end, hook to the left.

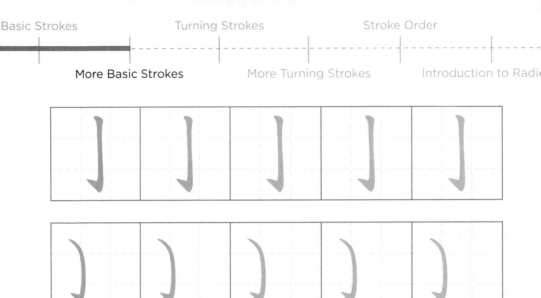

8. SHÙTÍ 竖提

Shùtí is the vertical line shù plus the tí stroke as a hook at the end. In other words, shùtí is like shùgōu, but flipped to the right and with a longer hook. However, the shùtí stroke appears less frequently in Chinese characters than the shùgōu stroke.

You can find shùtí in the character 长 zhǎng (*to grow*).

Note that the character 长 can also be pronounced cháng, in which case it means *long*.

Now practice writing the shùtí stroke by tracing the stroke in the boxes below. Remember to move your pen from top to bottom, and then hook to the right at the end.

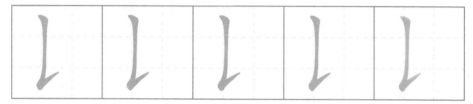

9. XIÉGŌU 斜钩

The xiégōu stroke can be viewed as a slanted version of the shùtí stroke. Simply start from the top, move diagonally to the lower left, and then finish the stroke with a hook to the right.

The xiégōu stroke can be found in the character 戈 gē (*spear*):

Now practice writing the xiégōu stroke by tracing the stroke in the boxes below. Remember to move your pen diagonally from top left to bottom right, and then hook to the right at the end.

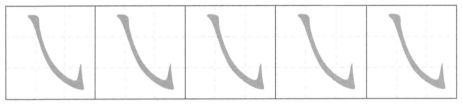

10. NÀ 捺

The nà stroke goes from top to bottom right. It is roughly the opposite of the "top to bottom left" piě stroke from Lesson 1. Like piě, nà can be tilted either more horizontally or more vertically depending on the character it's forming.

Nà can be found in the very common character 人 rén (*person, people*).

You can also find it in the character 天 tiān (*day, sky*).

Note that Chinese characters never contain more than one nà stroke. There can be two héng strokes in one character (as in 天 tiān), or two piě strokes, but never two nà.

Now practice writing the nà stroke by tracing the stroke in the boxes below, going from top to bottom right.

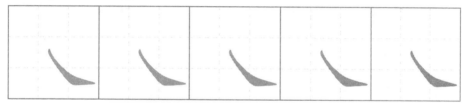

Exercise

Look at the following characters and see if you can identify the strokes we learned in this lesson and Lesson 1. Write down each stroke's pīnyīn name in the blank space provided. If you see more than one type of stroke in a character, make sure to write down the name of each one.

CHARACTER	STROKE NAME(S)
1. 天 tiān (*day, sky*)	
2. 小 xiǎo (*small*)	
3. 人 rén (*person, people*)	
4. 大 dà (*big*)	
5. 二 èr (*two*)	

CHARACTER	STROKE NAME(S)
6. 千 qiān (*thousand*)	

ANSWER KEY:

1. héng, piě, nà; 2. shùgōu, diǎn; 3. piě, nà; 4. héng, piě, nà; 5. héng; 6. piě héng, shù

Lesson 3

Turning Strokes

Turning strokes, or combined strokes, are made up of multiple turns of your pen. These strokes can be regarded as combinations of the basic strokes you learned in the previous lessons, plus some adjustments. However, and this is important, they are still written as one stroke. Here are five of them:

1. héngzhégōu 横折钩
2. héngzhé 横折
3. shùzhé 竖折
4. piězhé 撇折
5. shùwāngōu 竖弯钩

Let's take a closer look at each stroke.

11. HÉNGZHÉGŌU 横折钩

Héngzhégōu is a common stroke in Chinese writing. It is a combination of the horizontal line héng and the "vertical line + hook" shùgōu, but completed in one stroke. So, start by writing from left to right, then, without lifting your pen from the paper, turn downwards and add an upwards left hook at the end.

In handwriting, the shùgōu part is often tilted a bit to the left, but it is also fine to keep it strictly vertical. The "joint" that connects the horizontal héng part to the vertical shùgōu part can either be round or a perpendicular turn.

Héngzhégōu appears in many complex characters, but for now, we'll look at a few basic examples. For example, héngzhégōu can be found in the character 习 xí (*to study*).

It can also be found in 勺 sháo (*spoon*)

Now practice writing the héngzhégōu stroke by tracing the stroke in the boxes below. Don't forget to write from left to right, and then go down and add an upwards left hook at the end, all without lifting your pen or pencil from the paper.

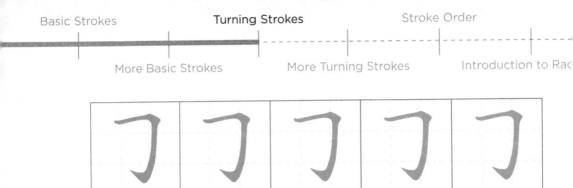

12. HÉNGZHÉ 横折

The héngzhé stroke is simply héngzhégōu without the gōu (*hook*). So write from left to right and then go down.

Héngzhé can be found the character 口 kǒu (*mouth*).

The héngzhé stroke is less common than the héngzhégōu stroke, and it can be difficult to differentiate the two when they are used to form a square, such as in the character 日 rì (*sun, day*):

So is that stroke héngzhé or héngzhégōu? Well, this is often a matter of debate. Just keep in mind that, in actual handwriting, either stroke is acceptable if you need to form a square in a character like 日 rì.

Let's look at another example of the héngzhé stroke. The character 书 shū (*book*), shown below, contains both the héngzhé and héngzhégōu strokes.

Now, practice writing the héngzhé stroke a few times by tracing the stroke in the boxes below.

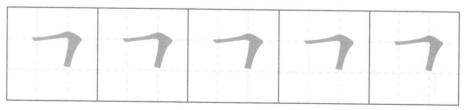

13. SHÙZHÉ 竖折

The shùzhé stroke is made up of the vertical line shù and the horizontal line héng. So you write from top to bottom and then go right.

Depending on the character it is forming, shùzhé can either be a short vertical line with a long horizontal line, or vice versa. For example, shùzhé is a short vertical line with a long horizontal line in the character 山 shān (*mountain*):

However, in the character 断 duàn (*to break off*), the stroke is a long vertical line with a short horizontal line:

Now practice writing the shùzhé stroke by tracing the stroke in the boxes below. Remember to draw the vertical line first and then turn right and draw the horizontal line.

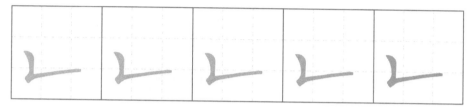

14. PIĚZHÉ 撇折

Piězhé is very similar to shùzhé. The piězhé stroke simply replaces the vertical line shù with the tilted line piě. So go from top to bottom left, then go horizontally to the right.

Piězhé can be found in the character 东 dōng (*east*):

It can also be found in the character 云 yún (*cloud*).

Note that sometimes piězhé ends by going diagonally down to the right, rather than going horizontally:

For example, it is written that way in the character 女 nǚ (*female, woman*):

Now practice writing both forms of the piězhé stroke a few times by tracing the stroke below. Remember to go from top to bottom left, then turn right and go horizontally or diagonally to the right, without lifting your pen or pencil from the paper.

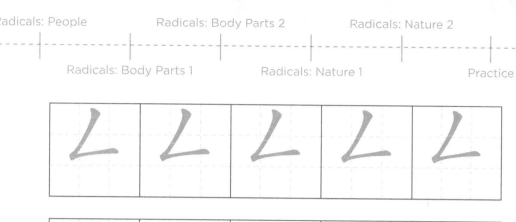

15. SHÙWĀNGŌU 竖弯钩

The shùwāngōu stroke is also like the shùzhé stroke, but with a round turn at the bottom left and a hook at the bottom right. In other words, it's a combination of the shù stroke, and a flipped, horizontal wāngōu stroke. So, write from top to bottom, make a rounded turn to the right, go horizontally, and then hook upwards.

The shùwāngōu stroke can be found in many Chinese characters. For example, you can find it in the character 已 yǐ (*already*).

You can also find it in the character 己 jǐ (*self*):

Notice that the only difference between 已 yǐ and 己 jǐ is the size of the opening in the upper left. In other words, the top of the shùwāngōu stroke in 已 yǐ starts closer to the top of the character, making the opening half closed, while the shùwāngōu stroke in 己 jǐ starts further down, leaving the opening completely open. These two characters highlight the importance of paying careful attention to how each Chinese character is written.

Practice writing the shùwāngōu stroke a few times by tracing the stroke in the boxes below. Remember to draw a round corner as you turn right and to finish with an upwards hook.

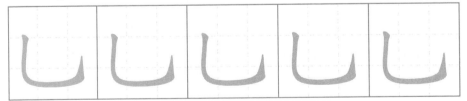

Exercise

Look at each of the following characters and see if you can identify the stroke we've learned in this lesson. Write down the stroke's pīnyīn name in the blank space provided. Only write down the strokes you've seen in this lesson.

CHARACTER	STROKE NAME
1. 方 fāng (*square*)	
2. 牙 yá (*tooth*)	
3. 车 chē (*car*)	
4. 巴 bā (*to hope*)	

ANSWER KEY:

1. héngzhégōu; 2. shùzhé; 3. piězhé; 4. shùwāngōu

Lesson 4

More Turning Strokes

Let's take a look at a few more turning strokes. These are the last strokes that will be introduced in this guide. By the end of this lesson, you will have learned the most commonly used brush strokes in Chinese writing.

Here are the turning strokes you will see in this lesson:

1. héngzhéwāngōu 横折弯钩
2. héngzhézhézhégōu 横折折折钩
3. shùzhézhégōu 竖折折钩
4. héngpiěwāngōu 横撇弯钩

Now let's break down each stroke.

16. HÉNGZHÉWĀNGŌU 横折弯钩

Héngzhéwāngōu starts with a version of héngzhé, followed by a flipped, horizontal wāngōu, which, as you know, is a curved form of the stroke shùgōu.

In other words, it starts with the horizontal line héng and then turns left, makes a wide round turn to the right, continues horizontally to the right, and ends with an upwards hook. Keep in mind that this is all one stroke. In other words, it should be written without lifting your pen or pencil from the paper.

Héngzhéwāngōu can be found in the character 忆 yì (*to remember*).

Now practice writing the héngzhéwāngōu stroke by tracing the stroke in the boxes below. Remember that you should write the entire stroke without lifting your pen or pencil from the paper.

17. HÉNGZHÉZHÉZHÉGŌU 横折折折钩

As you can probably tell, héngzhézhézhégōu is one of the more complex strokes.

It is essentially a combination of héngzhé and héngzhégōu, but written as one stroke. So start with the horizontal line héng and then go down, turn to the right and continue horizontally, then turn downwards and add an upwards left hook at the end.

Don't be intimidated by the long name of the stroke. The names of the strokes are not that important; just try to remember the shape of the stroke and the direction of your pen, and understand that it's written as one stroke.

One of the simplest characters that contains the héngzhézhézhégōu stroke is 仍 réng (*still*).

Now practice writing héngzhézhézhégōu by tracing the stroke in the boxes below.

18. SHÙZHÉZHÉGŌU 竖折折钩

Shùzhézhégōu is used quite frequently. It starts with the shù stroke, and then finishes off with the héngzhégōu stroke.

Shùzhézhégōu can be found in the character 弓 gōng (*bow – as in bow and arrow*).

Now practice writing shùzhézhégōu by tracing the stroke in the boxes below.

19. HÉNGPIĔWĀNGŌU 横撇弯钩

Héngpiĕwāngōu is the formal name for the stroke, but people usually refer to it as guàěr, or the *ear-shaped stroke*.

It starts with a shortened version of the héngpiĕ stroke, which is a combination of the strokes héng and piĕ:

It's then followed by the wāngōu stroke. So, in other words, start with a short horizontal héng and then go down diagonally to the left, turn slightly to the right, go down diagonally to the right, and then add an upwards left hook at the end.

Notice that héngpiěwāngōu resembles the shape of the number 3—or an ear, of course.

The héngpiěwāngōu stroke always has a shù stroke on its left side, as demonstrated in the character 队 duì (*team*).

Now, practice writing the héngpiěwāngōu stroke a few times by tracing the stroke in the boxes below.

Exercise

Look at each of the following characters and see if you can identify the stroke we've learned in this lesson. Write down the stroke's pīnyīn name in the blank space provided. Only write down the strokes you've seen in this lesson.

CHARACTER	STROKE NAME
1. 阳 yáng (*sun*)	
2. 亏 kuī (*deficit*)	
3. 亿 yì (*hundred million*)	
4. 乃 nǎi (*therefore*)	

ANSWER KEY

1. héngpiēwāngōu; 2. shùzhézhégōu; 3. héngzhéwāngōu; 4. héngzhézhézhégōu

Lesson 5

Stroke Order

Now that you've learned about strokes, let's take a look at how to use strokes to write an entire character.

Each Chinese character may contain anywhere from one to more than 30 strokes, and a certain order has to be followed in writing those strokes. Incorrectly ordered strokes can produce illegible or even incorrect characters.

Keeping that in mind, here are the general guidelines for stroke order when writing Chinese characters. There are exceptions, but these rules will allow you to write most Chinese characters.

Here are the rules for stroke order that you will see in this lesson:

1. Top to bottom
2. Left to right
3. Center before wings
4. Horizontal before intersecting vertical
5. Right-to-left diagonals before intersecting left-to-right diagonals
6. Enclosures before contents
7. Diǎn and other minor strokes last

Now let's look at each rule in detail.

20. TOP TO BOTTOM

In other words, you should always write the top stroke of a character first, and then move down from there.

For example, let's take a look at how to write the character 三 sān (*three*). 三 is made up of three héng strokes of varying lengths, with the shortest one in the middle. (If you need to review the héng stroke, see Lesson 1.)

As you can see, when writing 三, you start with the héng stroke at the top, then draw the one in the middle, and the one at the bottom comes last.

Of course, 三 is a very straightforward example. The "top to bottom" rule also applies to much more complex characters that have a top-down vertical structure.

Now practice writing by tracing the character in the box below. Remember to write from top to bottom.

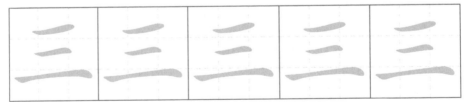

21. LEFT TO RIGHT

For most characters that have a left-to-right structure, you start from the left side, and then move on to the right side.

Take a look at how the character 八 bā (*eight*) is written:

八 has two strokes: a piě and a nà. Remember that piě goes from top to bottom left (Lesson 1), and nà goes from top to bottom right (Lesson 2). Notice that in the character 八, the piě on the left is written first, followed by the nà on the right.

Now let's practice. Trace the character in the box below, remembering to go from left to right.

22. CENTER BEFORE WINGS

Here is how to write the character 小 xiǎo (*small*):

As you can see, to write 小, you start with the shùgōu stroke in the middle, and then draw the diǎn stroke on the left and then the right.

In other words, with any vertically symmetrical character (like 小), the correct order would be to start with the component at the center, then write the component on the left and then the component on the right (following the "left to right" rule).

Now practice writing by tracing the character in the box below. Remember to draw the center before the wings, and then write from left to right.

23. HORIZONTAL BEFORE INTERSECTING VERTICAL

In general, a horizontal stroke precedes an intersecting vertical stroke.

For example, let's look at how to write the character 十 shí (*ten*). It has a simple structure: one héng stroke and one shù stroke.

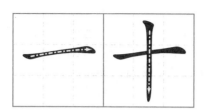

So the horizontal stroke (héng) is written before the intersecting vertical stroke (shù).

Now practice writing by tracing the character in the box below. Remember to draw the héng stroke before the shù stroke.

24. RIGHT-TO-LEFT DIAGONALS BEFORE INTERSECTING LEFT-TO-RIGHT DIAGONALS

For instance, you would write a piě stroke before an intersecting nà stroke. Again, remember that piě is a diagonal stroke that goes from top to bottom left (Lesson 1), and nà is a diagonal stroke that goes from top to bottom right (Lesson 2).

Let's look at an example. Here is how you write the character 文 wén (*language*):

So, to write 文, you start at the top with a diǎn stroke and then a héng stroke ("top to bottom" rule), and next you write a piě stroke and then intersect it with a nà stroke, following the intersecting diagonals rule that you just learned.

However, there are exceptions. Generally, if the character is considered to be "asymmetrical," or if one intersecting stroke is significantly longer than the other, then the order is reversed.

For example, in the character 戈 gē (*spear*), the xiégōu stroke (see the second box below) is written first, followed by the piě stroke (see the third box below).

Let's practice the "intersecting diagonals" rule, as well as the exception. Trace the characters in the boxes below, making sure to write the strokes in the correct order.

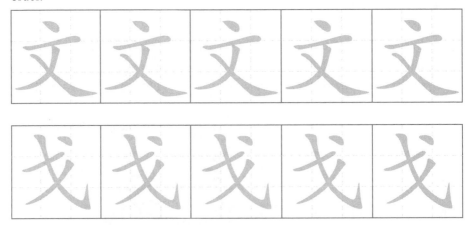

25. ENCLOSURES BEFORE CONTENTS

In other words, if a character has inside components that are enclosed by outside components, you would write the outside before the inside. However, you don't "close" the outer enclosure until the inside components have been completed.

That might sound a bit confusing, so let's look at an example. Take a look at how to write the character 回 huí (*to return*):

As you can see, you write most of the outer "square" before starting to write the inside "square." And the final héng stroke, which "closes" the outside square, is written last, once the inside square has been completed. (Also notice that both squares are written from "left to right" and "top to bottom.")

A similar example would be 田 tián (*field, farm*).

Notice that the inside component of this character also provides a good example of the "horizontal before intersecting vertical" rule.

Even if the outside component is not "closed," as in the character 同 tóng (*similar*), you would still write the outside components first.

Now let's practice the enclosure rule. Trace the characters in the boxes below, making sure to use the correct stroke order.

26. DIĂN AND OTHER MINOR STROKES LAST

Usually, the diǎn stroke (Lesson 1) and other minor strokes are written last. Minor strokes might include very short héng strokes.

Let's look at an example: 玉 yù (*jade*).

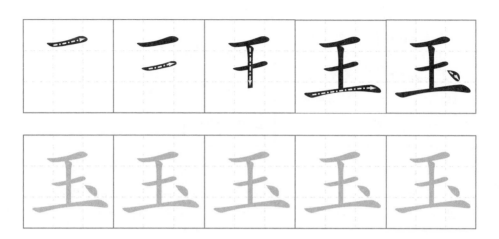

You can actually see several different rules in this character: "top to bottom," "horizontal before intersecting vertical" and finally, "diǎn last."

Note that if the diǎn or another minor stroke is inside an enclosure, diǎn is written second to last and the final stroke of the enclosure is written last.

Now let's practice:

Exercise

In the boxes below, fill in the strokes in the correct order. Make sure to write each stroke correctly, following what you learned in Lessons 1-4.

For example, if you saw:

You would write:

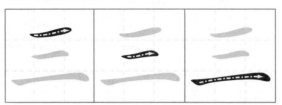

(Of course, the arrows are simply indicating the direction in which the stroke should be written; you don't actually have to write the arrows when you do the exercise.)

If you need to, first go back and review the strokes you learned in Lessons 1-4.

Ready?

1. 人 rén (*person, people*)

2. 二 èr (*two*)

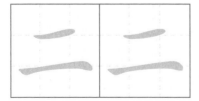

3. 干 gān (*dry*)

4. 口 kǒu (*mouth*)

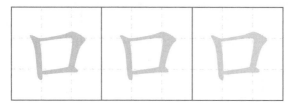

5. 日 rì (*sun, day*)

6. 天 tiān (*day, sky*)

7. 勺 sháo (*spoon*)

8. 水 shuǐ (*water*)

9. 月 yuè (*month*)

10. 国 guó (*country*)

ANSWER KEY:

1. 人 rén (*person, people*)

2. 二 èr (*two*)

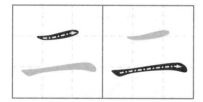

3. 干 gān (*dry*)

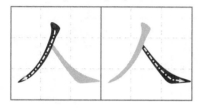

4. 口 kǒu (*mouth*)

5. 日 rì (*sun, day*)

6. 天 tiān (*day, sky*)

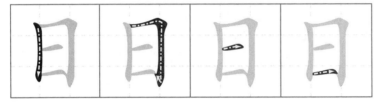

7. 勺 sháo (*spoon*)

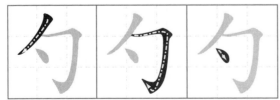

8. 水 shuǐ (*water*)

9. 月 yuè (*month*)

10. 国 guó (*country*)

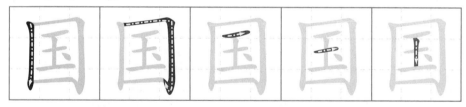

Part 2: Reading

Now that you've learned how to *write* characters, let's move on to learning how to *read* characters.

INDIVIDUAL CHARACTERS AND WORD UNITS

As you know, written Chinese is made up of a system of characters rather than an alphabet. Each syllable in the pīnyīn system represents one Chinese character. (See the Introduction for an overview of pīnyīn.)

For example, qiān is a syllable in pīnyīn. It represents one character and means *lead*. Bǐ is also a syllable, also representing one character, that refers to a general writing implement. Together, they form the word unit qiānbǐ (*pencil*) which is a word that is therefore made up of two characters.

In Chinese, zì means *character*—it refers to the individual characters in written Chinese. Cí means *word*, it refers to word units made up of two or more characters. Although individual characters/syllables such as qiān can and often do stand alone as individual "words," modern Chinese is also comprised of many word units like qiānbǐ. Therefore, many words that you learn in this guide and in the course as a whole will be made up of multiple syllables, and thus, multiple individual characters.

SPACING

When you read written Chinese characters, you will most likely notice that there are no spaces in the text, until you get to a comma or a period. For example:

当你读中文的时候，你会发现文句中没有空格，直到你达到一个逗号或者句号。

As you can see, there are no spaces between the characters above, except after punctuation. Note, however, that classical Chinese texts are not even punctuated.

Lesson 6

Introduction to Radicals

Although Chinese characters might look pretty complex at first, they are actually made up of parts called "radicals." Radicals can help you to decipher the meaning of a character. They also organize characters into specific groups, which can help you to remember more characters faster and look up characters in a Chinese dictionary.

There are 214 radicals in the current writing system, but only some of them are commonly used. In Part 2, we'll take an in-depth look at some of the most common radicals and how to use them to identify characters.

Here are the radicals that we will cover:

RADICAL	PĪNYĪN NAME	LITERAL ENGLISH TRANSLATION
亻	dān rén páng 单人旁	*single person radical*
彳	shuāng rén páng 双人旁	*double person radical*
女	nǚ zì páng 女字旁	*female radical*
口	kǒu zì páng 口字旁	*mouth radical*
目	mù zì páng 目字旁	*eye radical*

RADICAL	PĪNYĪN NAME	LITERAL ENGLISH TRANSLATION
阝	ěrduō páng 耳朵旁	ear radical
扌	tí shǒu páng 提手旁	hand radical
足	zú zì páng 足字旁	foot radical
辶	zǒu zhī páng/dǐ 走之旁/底	walking radical
日	rí zì páng 日字旁	sun radical
月	yuè zì páng 月字旁	moon radical
山	shān zì páng/tóu 山字旁/头	mountain radical
氵	sān diǎn shuǐ 三点水	three drops of water
艹	cǎo zì tóu 草字头	grass radical
土	tǔ zì páng 土字旁	earth/soil radical

For a complete list of radicals, see the back of the guide.

Now, before we examine individual radicals, let's talk more about how radicals work.

1. Each character contains one radical.

In addition to a radical, a character may contain other components, such as phonetic components that help indicate pronunciation. Since each character only has one radical, a component can be a radical in one character but a phonetic component in another character.

For instance, 禾 is a radical. However, in the character 和 hé (and, with, harmony), it's a phonetic component. The radical is 口.

2. Some radicals indicate the meaning of the character.

However, it is important to keep in mind that the radical may not indicate anything about the character at all, or at least not in an obvious way. A character may contain the "water" radical, for example, because that word originally came from the name of a river, even if the word has nothing to do with the river now.

3. All Chinese characters are organized into groups based on their radicals.

As a result, you actually use radicals to look up a character in a Chinese dictionary. Basically, radicals serve as a sort of indexing system.

In other words, there is usually a "radical index" at the beginning of a Chinese dictionary. To look up a character, find the character's radical in the first part of the index. The radicals are listed in order by number of strokes. So the simplest, one-stroke radicals are at the beginning, followed by more complex radicals, some of which may take more than twelve strokes to write. Once you find the radical, you will see a page number directing you to the second part of the index which lists all of the characters that contain that radical and where they can be found in the dictionary.

4. Essentially, there are two types of radicals.

First, there are radicals that can be both parts of characters and stand alone as full characters. One example of this type of radical is 日, known as the rì zì páng radical.

As a standalone character, 日 means *sun* or *day* and is pronounced rì.

However, it can also be found in many characters as a radical, such as in 春 chūn (*spring*).

Second, there are radicals that can never stand on their own; they can only serve as components of characters.

One example of this type of radical is 扌, known as the tí shǒu páng radical. It can be found in the character 打 dǎ (*to hit*):

Radicals of this type are often derived from a character. For example, 扌 is derived from the character 手 shǒu (*hand*).

Lesson 7

Radicals: People

In this lesson, we will look at three common radicals that are related to people.

RADICAL	PĪNYĪN NAME	LITERAL ENGLISH TRANSLATION
亻	dān rén páng 单人旁	*single person radical*
彳	shuāng rén páng 双人旁	*double person radical*
女	nǚ zì páng 女字旁	*female radical*

Now let's look at each one more in-depth.

1. 亻 **DĀN RÉN PÁNG 单人旁**

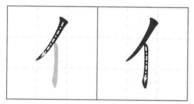

The 亻 radical has two strokes: a piě and a shù. It is derived from the character 人 rén (*person, people*), but it cannot be used as a standalone character.

The name dān rén páng literally means *single person radical*. As a result, it is often found in many characters whose meaning has something to do with people. For example:

你	他	住	休	什
nǐ	tā	zhù	xiū	shén

you (singular, informal)	he, him	to live in	to rest	what

In many cases, you can find certain logical connections between the radical and non-radical components of a character, and this can help you figure out the meaning of the character as a whole. For example, in the character 休 xiū (*to rest*), the non-radical part 木 mù means *wood* or *tree*. So, the character 休 indicates a 亻 person leaning against a 木 tree, thereby *resting*.

Note that 什 shén (*what*) is often combined with the character 么 me, which indicates a question, to form the common question word 什么 shénme (*what*).

2. 亍 SHUĀNG RÉN PÁNG 双人旁

The 彳 radical has just one more stroke than the 亻 radical, and its name shuāng rén páng literally means *double person radical*. It can be a standalone character, but it is rarely used as one. As a standalone character, it is pronounced chì and means *to step with the left foot*.

Characters containing 彳 are often loosely related to walking or people in the collective sense, but not always:

街	行	得	德
jiē	xíng	dé	dé
Street	to walk	to obtain	morality

The character 街 jiē (*street*) contains 土 tǔ, which means *soil* or *earth*. So, 彳 *people walking* on 土 *earth* means *street*.

Notice that the characters 得 dé (*to obtain*) and 德 dé (*morality*) have exactly the same pronunciation. This is similar to words like *four* and *for* in English, which are pronounced the same but have different meanings. As in English, they are usually easy to distinguish in context.

3. 女 NǙ ZÌ PÁNG女字旁

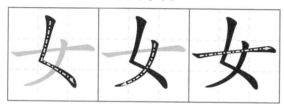

女 can be used as both a radical and a standalone character. As a standalone character, it means *woman* or *female* and is pronounced nǚ. Consequently, as a radical, 女 is often found in characters relating to women.

Note that when used as a radical, the héng stroke of 女 only goes halfway through and stops at the piě stroke:

Here are some characters that contain the 女 radical:

她	好	妈

tā	hǎo	mā
she, her	*good*	*mom*

The character for *good*, 好 hǎo, is actually a combination of 女 nǚ (*female, woman*) and 子 zǐ (*child*). So *good* is a *woman* and *child* together.

Note that the character 妈 mā (*mom*) contains the phonetic component 马 mǎ (*horse*).

Exercise
Match the characters on the left to the correct English translations on the right.

1. 好
2. 你
3. 妈
4. 街
5. 住

a. *mom*

b. *good*

d. *street*

e. *to live in*

f. *you (singular, informal)*

ANSWER KEY:
1. b; 2. f; 3. a; 4. d; 5. e

Lesson 8

Radicals: Body Parts 1
Now let's look at radicals that are related to the human body:

RADICAL	PĪNYĪN NAME	LITERAL ENGLISH TRANSLATION
口	kǒu zì páng 口字旁	*mouth radical*

RADICAL	PĪNYĪN NAME	LITERAL ENGLISH TRANSLATION
目	mù zì páng 目字旁	*eye radical*
阝	ěrduō páng 耳朵旁	*ear radical*

4. 口 KŎU ZÌ PÁNG 口字旁

口 is used as both a radical and a standalone character. As a standalone character, it is pronounced kǒu and means *mouth*. Notice that it actually looks like an open mouth.

Here are some examples that use the radical 口:

吃	听	吸	号	和
chī	tīng	xī	hào	hé
to eat	*to listen*	*to inhale*	*number, date*	*and, with, harmony*

The character 和 hé (*and, with, harmony*) is composed of the character for *grain*, 禾 hé, and the 口 mouth radical, suggesting that harmony is attained when people have enough grain to eat. The character 禾 hé also helps indicate pronunciation.

5. 目 MÙ ZÌ PÁNG 目字旁

目 is both a radical and a standalone character. The standalone character, pronounced mù, is mainly used in formal or classical writings to mean *eye*.

Most characters that contain the 目 radical are related to eyes or the act of looking. Here are some examples of characters that contain 目:

看	盯	睡	盲	眼	睛
kàn	dīng	shuì	máng	yǎn	jīng
to look at	*to stare at*	*to sleep*	*blind*	*eye*	*eye*

As you can see, the characters above are all closely related to the eyes.

In the character 睡 shuì (*to sleep*), the non-radical part, 垂 chuí, means *to droop*, so letting the eyes droop means *to sleep*. In the character 盲 máng (*blind*), the top part, 亡 wáng, means *to die*, so if the eyes die, the person is *blind*.

Note that the characters 眼 yǎn and 睛 jīng are mostly used together as a word unit to mean *eye*: 眼睛 yǎnjīng. Also note that the characters 盲 máng and 目 mù can be used together to form the word 盲目 mángmù, which means *aimless*.

6. 阝 ĚRDUŌ PÁNG 耳朵旁

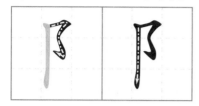

The name of the 阝 radical literally means *ear radical*, and the shape of the right portion of it does look like a human ear. Note that 阝 is not a standalone character. The full character for *ear* is 耳 ěr.

阝 can be used on either the left or right side of a character. Here are some examples:

阳	阴	队	附
yáng	yīn	duì	fù
sun, sunshine, masculine	*moon, cloudy, dark, female*	*line, queue, team*	*to attach*

邻	那	阻	陈
lín	nà/nǎ	zǔ	chén
neighbor	*that/how, which*	*to prevent*	*a family name, to exhibit, to explain*

For the character 阳 yáng (*sun, sunshine*), imagine the 日 rì (*sun*) hanging over someone's 阝 *ear*, and that means *sunshine*. Similarly, for the character 阴 yīn (*moon, cloudy, dark*), imagine a 月 yuè (*moon*) hanging over someone's 阝 *ear*, and that means *dark* or *cloudy*.

Also, you may be familiar with the Chinese philosophical term yin-yang. In characters, that term is written as 阴阳. In other words, *sun* and *moon*, or *sunshine* and *cloudy*, or *masculine* and *feminine*.

Note that the character 陈 chén is one of the most common family names in China.

Exercise

Match the characters on the left to the correct English translations on the right.

1. 吃
2. 睡
3. 陈
4. 和
5. 看

a. *and, harmony*

b. *to explain*

c. *to look at*

d. *to eat*

e. *to sleep*

ANSWER KEY:
1. d; 2. e; 3. b; 4. a; 5. c

Lesson 9

Radicals: Body Parts 2

Let's look at a few more radicals related to the human body.

RADICAL	PĪNYĪN NAME	LITERAL ENGLISH TRANSLATION
扌	tí shǒu páng 提手旁	*hand radical*
足	zú zì páng 足字旁	*foot radical*
辶	zǒu zhī páng/dǐ 走之旁/底	*walking radical*

7. 扌 TÍ SHǑU PÁNG 提手旁

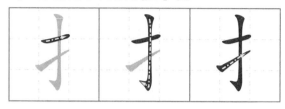

As you saw in Lesson 6, the 扌 radical is derived from the character 手 shǒu (*hand*). It cannot stand alone, but it can be found as a component of a lot of Chinese characters. Below are some examples:

打	扫	扔	把	报	抗
dǎ	sǎo	rēng	bǎ	bào	kàng
to hit	*to sweep*	*throw*	*to hold*	*to report, newspaper*	*to fight, to resist*

As you can see, all of the characters with a 扌 radical can be used as verbs.

Note that the characters 打 dǎ and 扫 sǎo can be used together to form the phrase 打扫 dǎsǎo, which still means *to sweep*. It depends on context whether you use 打扫 or simply 扫; they are sometimes interchangeable.

8. 足 ZÚ ZÌ PÁNG 足字旁

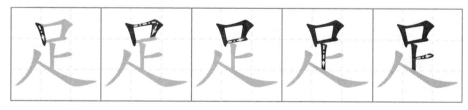

The 足 radical is also a standalone character meaning *foot*. When used as a standalone character, it is pronounced zú. And when used as a radical, it changes slightly in form:

Now here are some examples of 足 used as a radical:

跑	跳	踢	路
pǎo	tiào	tī	lù
to run	*jump*	*kick*	*road*

As you can see, the characters above all relate either to actions of the feet or what the feet stand on.

9. 辶 ZǑU ZHĪ PÁNG/DǏ 走之旁/底

The 辶 radical is not a standalone character. The name zǒu zhī páng literally means the *walking radical,* as it is derived from the character 之 and also looks like something that is "walking" or "zigzagging." The character 之 means *zigzag, winding,* or *S-shaped road,* but it is more often used to indicate possession, like the *'s* in English.

Notice that the printed style of the radical, or 辶, looks a little different from the handwritten style shown in the boxes above. When printed, the second stroke is a shù stroke, but in handwriting, it's a héngzhézhépiě stroke. The difference simply has to do with font styles, but when writing, you should always follow the handwritten style.

Here are some examples of characters that contain the 辶 radical:

追	退	逃	达	近	远
zhuī	tuì	táo	dá	jìn	yuǎn
to chase	*to retreat*	*to escape*	*to reach*	*near*	*far*

迟	这	送	进	迅	速
chí	zhè	sòng	jìn	xùn	sù
late	*this, here*	*to send*	*to enter*	*rapid*	*quick*

As you can see from their English translations, most of the characters above are more or less related to *walking* or other actions of the feet, with the exception of 这 zhè (*this*), which is the opposite of the character 那 nà (*that*) that you saw in the previous lesson.

Also, the other component is always sitting on top of the piě stroke.

Note that 迅 and 速 are often used together to form the word 迅速 xùnsù, which means *quickly* or *rapidly.*

Exercise

Match the characters on the left to the correct English translations on the right.

1. 路

2. 打

3. 近

4. 这

5. 远

a. *to hit*

b. *far*

c. *near*

d. *road*

e. *this*

ANSWER KEY:
1. d; 2. a; 3. c; 4. e; 5. b

Lesson 10

Radicals: Nature 1

In this lesson, we're going to look at a few radicals related to nature:

RADICAL	PĪNYĪN NAME	LITERAL ENGLISH TRANSLATION
日	rí zì páng 日字旁	*sun radical*
月	yuè zì páng 月字旁	*moon radical*
山	shān zì páng/tóu 山字旁/头	*mountain radical*

10.　日 RÍ ZÌ PÁNG 日字旁

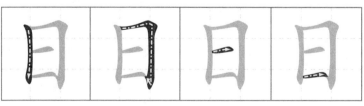

As you know from Lesson 6, 日 can be used as both a radical and a standalone character, in which case it means *sun* or *day* and is pronounced rì.

Most characters that contain 日 as a radical are related to time or weather. Since the sun is also associated with prosperity in Chinese culture, characters related to that theme often contain 日 as well.

早	晨	时	旧	昨
zǎo	chén	shí	jiù	zuó
early, morning	*dawn*	*time*	*old (not new), past*	*yesterday*

春	旱	是	星	旺
chūn	hàn	shì	xīng	wàng
spring	*drought*	*yes, to be*	*star*	*prosperous*

In the character 旱 hàn, the 日 *sun* on top of 干 gān (*dry*) indicates *drought*. In the character 旺 wàng (*prosperous*), a 王 wáng (*king*) stands next to the 日 *sun*, indicating prosperity.

Note that the characters 早 zǎo (*early, morning*) and 晨 chén (*dawn*) can be used together to form the word unit 早晨 zǎochén (*early morning*). Also, when you greet someone, you can use 早 zǎo by itself to say *Morning!*

Finally, make sure to remember the character 是 shì, which means both *yes* and the verb *to be*. As you can probably imagine, it's a very useful character to know!

11. 月 YUÈ ZÌ PÁNG 月字旁

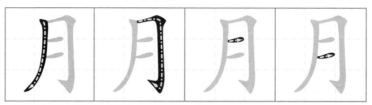

The 月 radical can also be used as a standalone character, in which case it is pronounced yuè and means *moon* or *month*.

Let's take a look at some examples of the radical 月.

朋	脸	脑	胖	肚	有
péng	liǎn	nǎo	pàng	dù	yǒu
friend	*face*	*brain*	*fat*	*belly*	*to have, there is/ there are*

Although 月 means *moon*, when used as a radical, it is mostly found in characters that are related to the human body, as you can see from the above examples.

Notice that péng simply contains two 月. So, essentially, two moons together means *friend*. Also note that to say *friend* in Chinese, 朋 péng is often combined with the character 友 yǒu, which also means *friend*: 朋友 péngyǒu (*friend*).

Like 是 shì, 有 yǒu is a very good character to remember. It's one of the most frequently used characters in Chinese.

12.　山 SHĀN ZÌ PÁNG/TOÚ 山字旁/头

山 is both a radical and a standalone character. As a standalone character, 山 means *mountain* and is pronounced shān. Notice that the shape of 山 also helpfully resembles mountains.

The radical 山 can be found in the following characters:

岁	岛	岸	出	峰
suì	dǎo	àn	chū	fēng
age, year	*island*	*bank, shore*	*to leave*	*peak, summit*

The character 峰 fēng can be used with the standalone character 山 to form the word unit 山峰 shānfēng (*mountain peak*).

The character 岁 suì (*age, year*) is composed of 山 and 夕 xī (*evening, sunset*). In other words, when the sun sets into the remote mountains, a *year* has passed and you are one year older in *age*.

The character for *island*, 岛 dǎo, is composed of 鸟 niǎo (*bird*) and 山. So, birds standing on a mountain means *island*.

Exercise

A. Match the characters on the left to the correct English translations on the right.

1. 是

2. 岁

3. 有

4. 早

5. 朋

a. *morning*

b. *to have*

c. *to be*

d. *friend*

e. *age*

B. Now let's review some of the characters you saw in previous lessons. Translate the following characters into English.

1. 路 _____

2. 远 _____

3. 吃 _____

4. 你_____

5. 好_____

ANSWER KEY:
A. 1. c; 2. e; 3. b; 4. a; 5. d
B. 1. *road*; 2. *far*; 3. *to eat*; 4. *you*; 5. *good*

Lesson 11

Radicals: Nature 2

In this lesson, we will continue to look at radicals that are related to nature:

RADICAL	PĪNYĪN NAME	LITERAL ENGLISH TRANSLATION
氵	sān diǎn shuǐ 三点水	*three drops of water*
艹	cǎo zì tóu 草字头	*grass radical*
土	tǔ zì páng 土字旁	*earth/soil radical*

13. 氵 SĀN DIǍN SHUǏ 三点水

The name of the 氵 radical, sān diǎn shuǐ, literally means *three drops of water*, and most of the characters that contain the 氵 radical are related to water. Note that 氵 is not a standalone character. The standalone character for *water* is 水 shuǐ.

You may have noticed that there is a difference in the radical's third stroke between the printed style 氵 and the handwritten style shown in the boxes above. As with the radical 辶 that you learned in Lesson 9, it's simply a font style. When you write the radical, make sure to follow the handwritten style.

Here are some examples using the radical 氵 :

汗	汉	汁	江	河	污

hàn	hàn	zhī	jiāng	hé	wū
sweat	*Chinese, Han*	*juice*	*large river*	*river*	*stain, dirt*

沉	浸	洗	油	活	泪
chén	jìn	xǐ	yóu	huó	lèi
to sink	*to soak*	*to wash*	*oil*	*to live*	*tears*

For the character 泪 lèi, 氵 *water* in the 目 *eye* means *tears*. For the character 活 huó, 氵 *water* on the 舌 shé (*tongue*) means that you *live*.

The character 汗 hàn (*sweat*) is composed of 氵 and 干 gān (*dry*). In other words, you sweat when it's too dry out.

The word 汉 hàn comes from the Han imperial dynasty of China, which ruled in China about two thousand years ago and got its name from the Han River, a branch of the Yangtze River (hence the use of the water radical). Most people in China belong to the Han ethnic group, and one word for the *Chinese language* is 汉语 hànyǔ, or literally, the language of the Han people.

The characters 沉 chén (*to sink*) and 浸 jìn (*to soak*) can be used together to form the word unit 沉浸 chénjìn, which means *to immerse* or *to be absorbed* in something.

14. ⺿ CǍO ZÌ TÓU 草字头

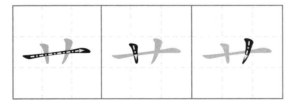

Like 冫 , ⁺⁺ cannot be used as a standalone character.

Characters that use the ⁺⁺ radical are usually related to grass or plants in some way. For example, take a look at the following characters that contain ⁺⁺:

草	花	节	芽
cǎo	huā	jié	yá
grass	*flower*	*festival, node*	*bud*

药	菜	蓝	艺
yào	cài	lán	yì
medicine	*vegetables, dish*	*blue*	*art, handicraft*

As you can see, most of the examples above are related to grass or plants.

In the case of the character 药 yào (*medicine*), the ⁺⁺ radical simply testifies to the fact that traditional Chinese medicines are mostly derived from plants. Also, it may seem as if the meaning of the character 蓝 lán (*blue*) has little to do with plants, but originally, 蓝 referred to the dark blue color of a plant that was used for dyeing clothes in ancient China.

The Traditional form of the Simplified character 艺 yì (*art, handicraft*) features two 木 mù (*wood, tree, plant*) components and another component that means *holding with hand*. As a result, the character indicates *holding a piece of wood*, meaning *handicraft* or *art*.

Note that the character 节 originally meant the node of a plant stem, but it is often used with the character 日 rì (*sun, day*) to refer to festivals: 节日 jiérì (*festival*).

Also note that the character 菜 cài (*vegetables, dish*) contains the character 采 cǎi (*to pick*). 采 cǎi depicts a 找 zhǎo (*hand*) picking off of a 木 mù (*tree, plant*).

15. 土 TŪ ZÌ PÁNG 土字旁

The 土 radical can also be used as a standalone character. As a standalone character, it is pronounced tŭ and means *earth, land,* or *dirt.* As a radical, it is mostly contained in characters that indicate location, space, or things that are considered "worthless."

For example:

地	在	垃	圾	坑
dì	zài	lā	jī	kēng
ground, land	*at, in, on*	*garbage*	*garbage*	*pit*

坏	均	坐	坚	场
huài	jūn	zuò	jiān	chǎng
bad, spoiled	*equal, average*	*to sit*	*strong, solid*	*open space, field*

The character 在 zài (*at, in, on*) is one of the most frequently used characters in Chinese. It is usually followed by words or phrases that indicate a location.

The characters 垃 lā and 圾 jī are almost always used together (垃圾 lājī) to mean *garbage* or something worthless.

Finally, notice that the character 坐 zuò (*to sit*) is made up of two 人 rén (*people*) sitting on the 土 (*earth*), thus its meaning: *to sit.*

Exercise

A. Match the characters on the left to the correct English translations on the right.

1. 菜   a. *to wash*

2. 汉   b. *festival*

3. 节   c. *at, in, on*

4. 洗   d. *Chinese*

5. 在   e. *vegetables*

B. Now let's practice what you learned in previous lessons. Identify the radical in each of the following characters and write it in the box provided.

1. 住 zhù (*to live in, to reside*)

2. 号 hào (*number, date*)

3. 打 dǎ (*to hit*)

4. 岁 suì (*age, year*)

ANSWER KEY:

A. 1. e; 2. d; 3. b; 4. a; 5. c

B. 1. 住 zhù (*to live in, to reside*)

2. 号 hào (*number, date*)

3. 打 dǎ (*to hit*)

4. 岁 suì (*age, year*)

Lesson 12

Practice

Welcome to the final lesson of the guide! Now that you've learned some of the most common radicals in Chinese, and been introduced to lots of new characters, let's take a look at a few simple sentences using the characters that you've learned.

Here are some additional characters and word units that you will see in the sentences below:

中国	请	那些	吗	的
Zhōngguó	qǐng	nàxiē	ma	de

China	please	those	indicates that the sentence is a question	sometimes used after adjectives

1. 你好吗?

Nǐ hǎo ma?

How are you? (lit., You are good?)

2. 她吃什么?

Tā chī shénme?

What is she eating? (lit., She eats what?)

3. 你有果汁和水。

Nǐ yǒu guǒ zhī hé shuǐ.

You have juice and water.

4. 他住在中国。

Tā zhù zài Zhōngguó.

He lives in China.

5. 看那些花!

Kàn nàxiē huā!

Look at those flowers!

6. 那些花是蓝的。

Nàxiē huā shì lán de.

Those flowers are blue.

7. 请坐!

Qǐng zuò!

Please sit!

8. 那是什么？

Nà shì shénme?

What is that? (lit., That is what?)

9. 那是街。

Nà shì jiē.

That is the street.

You've reached the end of the *Guide to Chinese Characters*! Congratulations! However, don't forget to practice as much as possible. That is the only way to become comfortable with strokes and familiarize yourself with deconstructing and identifying characters.

Practice writing individual strokes and then entire characters on your own. Review radicals, and try to identify characters on Chinese-language websites, newspapers, menus, and anywhere else you can find them.

Good luck!

Character Practice

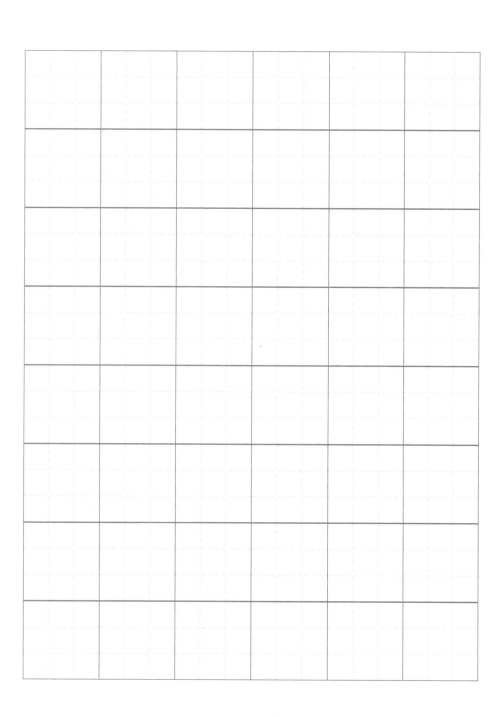

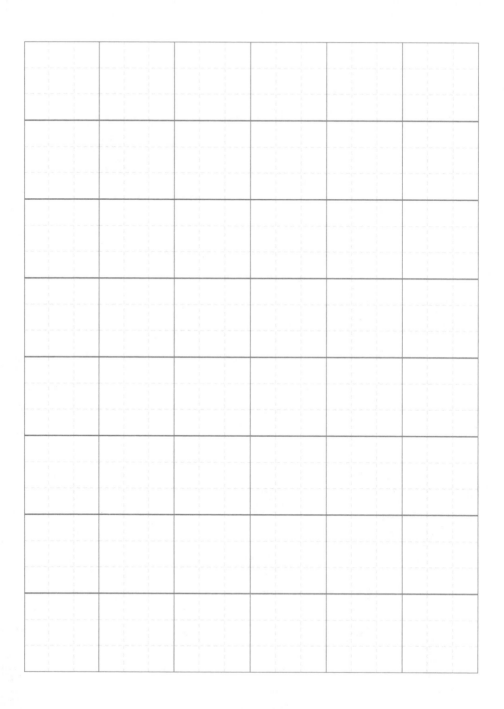